WORD WORLD

Let's Use

PRONOUNS

MARIE ROESSER

Enslow
PUBLISHING

Please visit our website, www.enslow.com. For a free color catalog of all our high-quality books, call toll free 1-800-398-2504 or fax 1-877-980-4454.

Library of Congress Cataloging-in-Publication Data

Names: Roesser, Marie, author.
Title: Let's use pronouns / Marie Roesser.
Description: New York : Enslow Publishing, [2023] | Series: Word world |
   Includes bibliographical references and index.
Identifiers: LCCN 2021044923 (print) | LCCN 2021044924 (ebook) | ISBN
   9781978527089 (library binding) | ISBN 9781978527065 (paperback) | ISBN
   9781978527072 (set) | ISBN 9781978527096 (ebook)
Subjects: LCSH: English language–Pronoun–Juvenile literature.
Classification: LCC PE1261 .R66 2023 (print) | LCC PE1261 (ebook) | DDC
   428.2–dc23/eng/20211122
LC record available at https://lccn.loc.gov/2021044923
LC ebook record available at https://lccn.loc.gov/2021044924

Portions of this work were originally authored by Kate Mikoley and published as *Let's Learn Pronouns!*. All new material this edition authored by Marie Roesser.

First Edition

Published in 2023 by
Enslow Publishing
29 E. 21st Street
New York, NY 10010

Designer: Katelyn Reynolds
Interior Layout: Rachel Rising
Editor: Therese Shea

Photo credits: Cover, pp. 1–4, 6, 8, 10, 12, 14, 16, 18, 20, 22–24 iadams/Shutterstock.com; Cover, p. 1 Faberr Ink/Shutterstock.com; Cover, p. 1 Illerlok_xolms/Shutterstock.com; Cover, p. 1 LimitedFont/Shutterstock.com; pp. 5, 21 Lamai Prasitsuwan/Shutterstock.com; p. 7 wavebreakmedia/Shutterstock.com; p. 9 Africa Studio/Shutterstock.com; p. 11 LightField Studios/Shutterstock.com; pp. 13, 17 Pixel-Shot/Shutterstock.com; p. 15 pixelheadphoto digitalskillet/Shutterstock.com; p. 19 Malenkka/Shutterstock.com.

Printed in the United States of America

Some of the images in this book illustrate individuals who are models. The depictions do not imply actual situations or events.

CPSIA compliance information: Batch #CSENS23: For further information contact Enslow Publishing, New York, New York, at 1-800-398-2504.

Find us on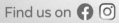

CONTENTS

Words in the glossary appear in **bold** type the first time they are used in the text.

NOUNS AND PRONOUNS

A noun is a word used for a person, place, or thing. Pronouns are words that **replace** nouns. The words in the colorful boxes on the next page are pronouns. Read on to learn more. The questions in this book will help you. Check your answers on page 22.

Pronoun

Subject	Object
I	
You	Me
We	You
They	Us
He	Them
She	Him
It	Her
	It

SINGULAR OR PLURAL?

Pronouns can be singular or plural. "Singular" means one person or thing. "Plural" means more than one. Make sure you use the right pronoun to replace the noun.

In the sentence below, which pronoun could replace the underlined words, *They* or *He*?

The kids jumped.

CHANGING IT UP

Pronouns keep us from being too **repetitive**. Repeating a noun can sound strange. Here's an example:

Mia loves school. Mia walks. Mia smiles.

Which pronoun could replace "Mia" in the second and third sentences, *She* or *You*?

SO USEFUL!

Some pronouns do a lot! When talking to one person or several, you'll use the pronoun *you*. The word *it* is a pronoun that stands for a nonliving object. But *it* is used for an animal or idea too.

Which pronoun could replace the noun "book," *they* or *it*?

SUBJECT PRONOUNS

Subject pronouns act as the subject of the sentence. The subject is doing the action of the sentence. *He, she, it, they*, and *we* are subject pronouns. Read this sentence:

> They fly kites.
>
> What subject pronoun is doing the action?

OBJECT PRONOUNS

Some pronouns receive the action in a sentence. They're called object pronouns. *Me, him, her, us*, and *them* are object pronouns. Read the sentence below:

> Emma hugs her.
>
> What object pronoun is receiving the action?

POSSESSIVE PRONOUNS

Some pronouns show ownership. These are called **possessive** pronouns. *His, hers, mine, ours,* and *yours* are examples. Let's see one of these pronouns in a sentence:

This shirt is mine.

What pronoun tells who owns the shirt?

17

NOUN FIRST

When you write, make clear what noun the pronoun replaces. Use the noun first. Then replace it with a pronoun. Which pair of sentences below clearly tells us what *it* stands for?

A. I love it. It is yellow.
B. I love my bike. It is yellow.

MANY MORE PRONOUNS

What, who, and *which* are pronouns that help with asking questions. *Which* have you used? *This, that, these,* and *those* can act as pronouns too. And *these* aren't the only ones. Don't forget *anyone* and *everyone*. After all, *everyone* needs pronouns!

Pronoun

Subject	Object
I	Me
You	You
We	Us
He	Him
She	Her
It	It
They	**Them**

GLOSSARY

possessive Belonging to someone.
repetitive Saying something again and again.
replace To take the place of something.

ANSWER KEY

p. 6: They
p. 8: She
p. 10: it
p. 12: They
p. 14: her
p. 16: mine
p. 18: B

FOR MORE INFORMATION

BOOKS

Cleary, Brian P. *I and You and Don't Forget Who: What Is a Pronoun?* Minneapolis, MN: Lerner Publications, 2022.

Dahl, Michael, and Lauren Lowen. *Pronouns Say "You and Me!"* North Mankato, MN: Picture Window Books.

Heinrichs, Ann. *Pronouns*. Mankato, MN: The Child's World, 2020.

WEBSITES

Parts of Speech
www.abcya.com/parts_of_speech.htm
This game helps you spot parts of speech, including pronouns.

The Pronouns
grammaropolis.com/pronoun.php
Check out this fun pronoun site.

INDEX